THE DOGS
IN MY
HOME

Tips
on
Handling
More
Than
One Dog

F. F. KOTES

ISBN 0-9615541-9-3

Library of Congress LC 91-067327

Copyright 1991 by Valley House
          Books
An Imprint of Martin Management
          Books

All rights reserved, including the right to reproduce this book, or parts thereof, except for the inclusion of brief quotations in a review or article.

Valley House Books, Martin Management Books,
Box 119, R.R. #1, Wailuku, Hawaii 96793

TABLE OF CONTENTS

		Page
	INTRODUCTION	1
1.	**YOU AND YOUR DOGS**	5
2.	**PRACTICAL MATTERS** The Law, Facilities, Sleeping, Feeding, Health and First Aid, First Day and Night	13
3.	**NEEDS OF NEWCOMER DOGS** Areas for Assessment, the Schedule, Exercise and Play, Housebreaking, Car Riding, Grooming	27
4.	**MULTIDOG ADJUSTMENT** After Adjustment, Games Dogs Play with Owners, Cat and Dog Adjustment, Children and Multidog Adjustment	45
5.	**SEX AND BREEDING** Not Breeding, Breeding, Puppies	57
6.	**TRAINING AND TRICKS** Individual Dog Obedience, ABC'S of Training, Pack Training, Tricks	65
7.	**CONCLUSION**	75
	ABOUT THE AUTHOR	77

INTRODUCTION

You have a much loved dog who is a family pet, is fairly well trained, usually happy, and doubles as a watch dog, with whom you have a special rapport.

Then, through your deliberate decision, or a set of circumstances, you suddenly enlarge your personal dog population to two or even more. How you acquired those newcomer dogs may vary widely.

Perhaps you have a pedigreed or mixed breed female who had a litter of puppies, and you decided to keep one or two of them.

You may have received a pedigreed dog for your birthday or for Christmas with show potential... exactly what you wanted.

You may have lost your resident dog and long-time friend, and then decided to bring home two new puppies to fill the family need for a pet.

Because your resident dog seems lonely and bored, you may have gone to a breeder or animal shelter to select a dog who you hope will provide friendship and exercise for the older pet.

Perhaps you are a "back-yard breeder" and want to find a suitable mate for your pedigreed or mixed breed dog. You are sure you can find good homes for the puppies in your area.

Security around your house may need to be increased and the job is really too much for one pet alone.

Or, fate steps in and gives you another dog.

That abandoned pup you saw sitting along-side the highway, sad and forlorn, hope all but gone. He lets you approach him, wags his tail a bit, and sighs. You put him in your car, determined to take him to the animal shelter in the morning. However, after feeding, brushing, and a good night of sleep, he really seemed like such a "special" dog, that somehow he never got there. Now, after informing the police and waiting a required period of time, he has a home with you!

Perhaps that new dog just wandered into the yard, eyes begging for help.

Perhaps your child arrived home after school with a cute young dog trailing behind him who "just followed him home"...his next question, of course, being "Can I keep him Mom? Please?"

Maybe you know a neighborhood dog who already plays with your dog and is seriously neglected by its owner. You finally volunteer to take in the dog, of whom you have grown fond, and the owner lets him go.

Whatever the circumstances, you now have more than one dog!

More than one will be twice as much fun, but more than twice the number of problems. They will cost double the amount in food and veternarian bills. Further, they will take up twice as much time and energy on your part to make them into the kind of dogs you want them to be as members of your family.

Each circumstance brings with it the special problems stemming from the unique background of the newly acquired dog, his breed characteristics, his life experiences thus far, as well as your own behavorial expectations for him, and the background and character of your resident dog.

Many people think that taking care of an added dog is simply a matter of providing two of everything ...two dinners, two beds, and so on. They often learn to their surprise that what "works" with one dog does not necessarily "work" with two or more dogs.

Before making the decision to assume the added responsibility of another dog, consider the alternative of actively cultivating more dog play sessions with the dogs in the neighborhood or those casually encountered in the park or on the beach. If you operate on a tight time schedule, this may be the only practical solution. Dogs take time and energy. More dogs take more time and energy. To get dogs out of doors today, many areas have dog walking services that are proving very helpful to busy owners also.

When making the decision about adding another dog ask yourself:

Do I want another dog?
Do I want this particular dog?

If your emotional response to the dog you are considering is not strong, don't keep him.

But, if you know that THIS DOG is going to be YOUR DOG, you won't mind the extra work, time, and energy required to make him a valued family pet.

This book is about making your life with the dogs in your home easier and more fun as well, both for you and your pets.

Having more than one dog in your family is different than having just one in many ways. Although individual dogs and circumstances differ, some generalizations can be made that will be helpful to the multidog owner.

YOU AND YOUR DOGS

Most dogs today are kept as pets, friends, and companions. Some do work, such as hunting dogs and police dogs. Some are highly skilled and trained to help the disabled to lead more productive lives. Some are kept primarily for protection. Others are kept primarily for breeding. All should be kept as pets also. The way you see your own relationship with your dogs determines what you do to train them and forms the basis of your environment for living with them.

But why do we keep a dog instead of something else? Basically, we prize dogs for their honesty and the openness of their response to us, in a much too superficial world. They are a bit of nature itself, bringing us down to reality and sharing with us the pure joy of living for its own sake. They will give us a devoted love if we deserve it, by treating them as they should be treated, i.e. as whole living animals with instincts and needs that must be met in order for them to be mentally alert and physically healthy. Protecting and caring for the whole animal as though it were a cherished family member is important.

Dogs are not toys...although they love to play with you.

They are not ornaments..although many are beautiful or magnificent of stature.

They are not inanimate objects. They are living creatures with feelings, personalities, needs, and emotions of their own.

They are not clowns...although many can perform tricks.

Dogs are not security alarm systems...although most will protect you and the home they live in with loyalty and consistency.

The more you can see your dog as a WHOLE, the more you will tend to treat him as a member of the family and as an active participant in your life and the lives of the family members who accept him.

He will share in your joys and sorrows with his own happiness and sadness, giving you a lifetime of selfless devotion. Can anyone do more?

You got your first dog because he was "special" to you. Throughout your dogs life, he must remain just as special to you. A bonding that usually begins in puppyhood, should become deeper over the years.

You will want to have this special relationship with every dog you bring into your family group. To do this you should understand each individual dog, as well as the basic standards of dog care. Some initial analysis and evaluation is especially critical with full grown newcomer dogs.

Unfortunately, in their relationships with dogs, some people have the high initial hope that they have found the perfect pet for them, only to be disappointed.

The relationship sours because of some negative experience with the pet. A puppy may mess up the carpet or may bite you with needle sharp puppy teeth, or a grown dog may not obey you at some critical time and embarrass you in public with his behavior.

Never give up on your relationship with your dogs and never take it for granted. Dog ownership is not for the thin-skinned. No dog is perfect. He WILL embarrass you sometimes, and he WILL misbehave.

How well adjusted he turns out to be will be due in most part to the kind of care he gets from you throughout his lifetime. You are the one who shapes his daily environment. He can turn out to be a marvelous pet, just an average dog, or a shy, rejected creature, trying to survive from day to day.

Not everything is up to you however. Every owner must start with an understanding of the basic nature of dogs.

Dogs are pack animals who like to live in groups. You are a part of their group. If you have only one dog, the two of you are his group.

As leader of a pack, you protect the dogs and make sure they survive. Within the pack there will be a pecking order established with some more dominant and some more submissive dogs. Dogs will claim a territory, usually their yard, which they will defend. Strangers and other dogs entering the dog pack territory will be challenged and sometimes attacked unless the leader intervenes.

As the leader and protector of the group of dogs you own, you send out verbal and nonverbal messages to your dogs daily about how you feel about them, how you want them to behave, whether you are happy or sad, apprehensive or disturbed.

A happy owner tends to have a happy dog. Thus the owner should try to send positive upbeat messages to pets, both to keep their attitudes positive for training purposes and to keep them happier. Keep your tone of voice happy. Train and give commands with a positive, firm, but happy tone of voice. A stern or sad voice should be saved for misbehavior, since it arouses anxiety in the pet.

Your dogs communicate with you too. They bark when protecting, howl when sad, yelp when in pain, and whine when they want something or are being left out of something. They also use body language a great deal, both with other dogs and with people.

As the leader of your dogs you can be a good leader or a poor one.

A good leader has the respect of his dogs. He or she is fair, protects his pack, provides for their needs, and has fun with them. He trains them, socializes them, spends time with them, pets them, and loves them. He will be loved in return.

A poor leader rules his pack through fear and intimidation. His dogs never know whether they will be yelled at, hit, rejected or neglected, depending on his mood. Their needs are met on a hit and miss basis, their exercise curtailed, seldom if ever groomed, and never bathed.

Or perhaps they are over protected and have no contact with the outside world. They may be kept almost entirely in a house or apartment, or kept in a back yard all of the time with nothing to do but fight among themselves to pass the time. This owner will be neither respected nor loved by his pets.

Abuse can take many forms which can be devastating for pets who live with neurotic owners on a daily basis. Fortunately, the minor behavorial quirks of some owners can be adjusted to by their dogs without too much difficulty and with little or no damage to the dog.

In other cases, dogs are deprived of their basic needs by an ignorant or uncaring owner, and does suffer mental or physical harm to some extent, which may make him neurotic or vicious.

The importance of meeting those basic dog needs cannot be stressed too strongly. They are:

. the need for good food and clear water daily.

. a shelter that is warm and dry , inside or outside in a kennel.

.daily exercise and play for physical and mental health, and to alleviate boredom.

.ample walks for elimination purposes.

.training in basic obedience to help give the dog a sense of order in his life, and to enable you to take him out more places.

.problem prevention and corrective attention to problems that already exist.

.your love and affectionate attention.

All of these are basic dog needs. Without them he is never going to develop into the kind of dog you want him to be, and he will never have a truly warm and loving relationship with you...that sense of oneness that some owners develop with their pets.

As you welcome a new pet to your home, take a few moments to examine your present care of the dog or dogs you now have. Are you satisfied with it? Does it seem to provide you with excellent quality pets or can you see room for improvement? This is the time when changes can be made more easily in the way you do things with your dogs, since any new dog brings change into the home situation.

Start with thinking through the best overall schedule for all your dogs. A planned schedule is desirable because it establishes a pattern, and allows dogs to anticipate the important things in their day with accurate expectations, thus lowering anxiety. A dog who never knows when or if he is going to eat is worrying about it constantly. He is building up tension and always has behavorial problems. Your schedule for them should include all of the basic needs mentioned above.

Once the schedule has been established, stay with it for a few weeks. Then vary what you do <u>within</u> the schedule. For example, if you always exercise your dogs by taking them for a long walk in the park at 7:00 am, vary <u>where</u> it is taken or the direction you walk into the park. But continue to take your walk with them at that time. This kind of variation for every activity occasionally, will make activities more enjoyable for both you and the dogs. Better quality time is more fun!

Another important point is in the treatment of the dogs on a daily basis. Make your environment as easy to get along in as possible. thus creating a happier environment, by minimizing the number of traumas the dog must go through to get along well.

Give them as much freedom to do what they want to do as possible within a defined pattern, and don't try to train them to do things that are contrary to the nature of the dog. For example, his natural instincts may tell him to do his elimination outside his own yard on the neighborhor's lawn. He should be trained to eliminate in his own yard, but not trained to try and use the toilet...which is too far from his natural instinct and capacity.

In your daily treatment of your dogs, be fair, patient, gentle, and firm. Don't yell or strike a dog for minor infractions. Save that very occasional hit for a serious biting situation or deliberate disobedience in an adult dog, and then hit only once combined with a verbal "no, no". To be effective, this correction must be done when you catch the dog actually misbehaving, not after it has happened and he has already forgotten about it. Often a stern "no, no" is all it takes to correct the behavior.

Some dog problems can best be dealt with by letting the dog outgrow them. This passive owner response is best with younger dog problems in which prevention is the key, i.e. the provision of rawhide bones as a substitute for the dog chewing everything in sight.

Anticipating problems and changing the circumstances to deal with situations before thry occur will save the owner and the dogs trauma and grief. Although not everything can be anticipated, an experienced dog owner can foresee trouble and should always be alert to ways to avoid it. This is especially true in multidog households.

Anticipate and prevent the problems you can see, substitute activities for smaller behavorial infractions with only mild or no correction for the dogs, ignore other problems which are likely to go away by themselves, and give direct active correction only for serious or deliberate misbehavior for adult dogs. For puppies, verbal scolding "no, no" is sufficient. Remember that trauma and negative personality effects should be avoided for happy dogs with positive attitudes.

At the same time, the dogs must know you are the leader and you set the rules for behavior, not they themselves.

With your dog pack, treat all dogs fairly and equally, but also differently according to their individual needs. Give each time alone with you, but do the things that are required by each dog for his best development also.

Although individual situations vary, the basic idea of fairness does not. Good treatment creates a well balanced harmony between the dogs, the owner, and the family in a pleasant environment, which is its own reward of happy living.

PRACTICAL MATTERS

THE LAW

Before you can realistically plan for that second or additional dog, you should review the legal requirements in your area, including leash laws, liability, and licensing requirements.

Check on the number of dogs allowed one owner in your residential or rural area. Although there may be no limit to the number one owner can have, they must be cared for properly or they can be taken from you. Dogs must be kept healthy, well fed, and disease free, and not be a nuisance in the community.

A dog license is usually required and the tag should be worn for identification if he gets lost.

Damage done by your dogs is usually the full responsibility of the owner who has failed to control his dogs, including biting, chasing and killing livestock, and property damage.

Don't let your dogs bark or howl excessively. Don't let them chase joggers, cars, or bicycles or lunge at those walking on the public streets.

Don't let them bite or harass service people who come to your home, such as mailmen, meter readers and others.

It is best to keep your dogs on your own property, where they are free to run and play in safety.

When they are off your property they should be on a leash.

Learn local laws regarding the curbing of dogs for elimination purposes outside your own yard.

Most people who have more than one dog, and certainly more than three, have houses with some sort of kennel facility. For their own development and the enhancement of rapport between dogs and their owner, the use of kennel facilities should be tempered with daily contact with their family and living experiences inside the house, as well as play in the yard and walks on leash with you outside the yard.

With this combination environment, the dogs will be healthier and happier, as well as better adjusted and better mannered.

FACILITIES

The very best solution to trying to keep your dogs on your own property is a fenced-in yard. An alternative is kennel facilities with a large fenced-in exercise enclosure for them.

Trying to train your dogs to remain within the boundries of your unfenced yard just does not work. If they run loose you run the risk of a car accident and the loss of a beloved pet , someone picking up your dog to keep himself as a stray he has found, or even the local animal shelter removing the dog as a stray.

Aside from certain toy breeds, having several dogs together inside the house when you go out, or even when you are there, does not work well. Full of energy, they will play, bark, and chase one another, jump over and onto furniture, and tear up things. The house is not the place for a pack of potentially destructive dogs.

Neither should dogs be confined to small spaces either alone or together. They need to move around and will fight and become irritable quickly if confined for even short periods.

It is also inhumane to tie a dog on a short line outside or inside for more than about an hour. Even on a long line he must have the capacity to walk around for the sake of his circulation and muscles and to relieve himself when he wants to do so.

Kennels need not be especially built. In colder climates many basements have been converted into kennels, the warmth and dryness an added advantage, with exercise yards an addition.

Others build dog runs with standard kennels at the end of the run. These should be made of galvanized steel fencing 6-10 ft wide and 12-20 ft long, depending on the breed of the dogs, with a cement surface for easy cleaning.

The dog house at the end of the run should be well off the ground so there is no water problem; it should be small enough to hold the dogs warmth and large enough for him to move around in. The roof should slope with an overhang at the front to keep the rain out. A hinge on the roof helps easy cleaning. The amount of shade needed in the summer is important, as well as the circulation of air.

The yard and kennel area should be free of debris and cleaned every day. Paints, garden tools, and any potentially dangerous plant should be removed from curious puppies and dogs.

You will keep your relationships with your neighbors friendlier if you make your dogs good citizens of the area by NOT allowing them to roam outside their yard and destroy flowers, eliminate on the yard adjacent, or growl at people on their own property. "Good fences make good neighbors" has been proven true in many situations.

The number of individual facilities will depend on the number of dogs you have, their breeds and their ages, as well as whether they are male or female.

In general, there should be a separate facility for special use by a mother and puppies, a sick or injured dog, or a female in heat. These dogs should not be housed near aggressive males since they will cause anxiety or fighting.

New dogs should not be housed with resident dogs, since they sometimes will fight with and kill a newcomer.

Females are best kenneled with females and males with males, so the males are not competing for the attentions of the female.

Puppies should never be placed with male dogs, even the father, since they may injure and kill them.

Finally, any dogs who do not get along well should never be housed together, male or female.

Many owners rotate spending the evening inside the house with each dog in turn. This helps socialization.

One further word needs to be said about the protection of your much loved pets. It is unfortunate that not everyone is trustworthy and ethical, but they are not. Not everyone likes dogs, and some see the dogs of other people as a way to make money for themselves. Don't let your dogs be stolen and resold to new owners, used in scientific experiments in laboratories, made to fight in gamblers dog fights, or slaughtered in some back yard and eaten as a delicacy..as some ethnic groups do in Hawaii for instance. Nationally and at the state levels these cases are well documented.

You must provide for your dogs safety in your absence. Gates should be kept locked to dog enclosures and dogs not kept accessible to people on the streets. Dog enclosures should have tops so dogs cannot climb out or children or others climb in. When you are home be aware of barking that signals an intruder. Your supervision can save you heartache.

MORE SLEEPING ARRANGEMENTS

Multidog owners usually have kennel facilities for pets to sleep in as just described. If you have only one dog and are going to own another one, decide where he will sleep, inside or outside.

Your resident dog may well have been permitted to sleep in the house at the foot of your bed. This will not work with two dogs.

Even if they are adjusted to one another and play together outside, the resident will not let the newcomer come up onto the foot of the bed with him, and the newcomer will not sleep on the floor if the other dog is on the bed. There will be growling, snapping, scuffling, and even fighting on and around the bed during the night, with you in the middle of it.

Avoid this competitive situation by allowing only
the resident dog in your room. If you banish him too
his jealousy of the newcomer dog will intensity, and
he may resent you as well. Make adequate sleeping
arrangements for the newcomer dog in another room,
depending on his age requirements. For example,
a puppy will need his own bed-box surrounded by
newspapers probably near some other adult.

Two adult dogs who must sleep in the same room may
need to be separated by tying to sturdy pieces of
furniture, so they do not start to play or fight
during the night. Rope should be at least six feet
long and dogs should be secured as far apart as
possible on their individual beds. They should be
free within the house or outside until time for
sleep.

Whether inside or outside, make your dogs as comfortable as possible. There will be less walking
around during the night, and they will develop
fewer callouses which can cause serious problems
on the elbows.

FEEDING

Just as most people do, dogs like to eat. It is the
responsibility of the owner to see that what his
pet eats contributes all that he needs to be a
healthy, strong, and attractive animal.

The basic standard for feeding is:
    .weaning to 12 weeks - 4 feedings a day
    .3-6 months - 3 feedings
    .6 months to 1 year - 2 feedings
    .over 1 year - 1 or 2 feedings

What to feed depends on your dog requirements as well
as your own preference.

Puppies should have a good quality puppy food, which meets their nutritional needs.

Adult dogs should have a good quality adult food, while older dogs over seven or eight years should be fed senior dog food if they show any sign of digestive upset.

The food you offer the dog determines his condition and resistance to disease. You should offer a nationally known high quality food at all times for best results.

I have found the main meal for adult dogs fully satisfying with a combination of dry food added to canned food, plus meat, and mixed together. Vegetables such as carrots or peas can be mashed and also added occasionally. If the dog is underweight, boiled potatoe, spaghetti, or a little bread can also be added. For variety broth, cottage cheese, or the yellow of an egg can also be added at some time.

By varying the flavor of the canned portion of the dog food, appetite can be kept keen. Dry food can also be mixed with another type , perhaps of a different size.

The meat given can be beef, lamb, liver, heart, kidney, or fish without bones. Chicken without bones is also relished occasionally.

The amounts of the food given depend on the age of the dog and the number of feedings it receives. The package will provide all needed information. However, this is only a guide. Your dogs will eat more in a cold climate,when they are growing, when they are pregnant or nursing, or when they are working or hunting. If they are older or sedentary, or neutered, they need less food.

Feeding should be done according to the schedule you have done for the overall care of your dogs. Regular hours help your dogs physically and decrease their anxiety over food. They should be taken out immediately after eating.

If milk is given it should be diluted evaporated milk which causes fewer digestive upsets. I believe milk should be given, if possible, because of the nutritional value, Expert opinions vary on this.

As indicated in the schedule, puppies eat several meals a day. These can be varied between puppy chow and diluted milk in the morning, a little canned puppy food at 11:00am, puppy chow and canned puppy food and meat at 3:00pm, and a final meal about 8:00pm to hold him over until morning.

Baby cereal can be used for puppies occasionally, and their food can be supplemented with a little cod liver oil for dry skin. Vitamins and calcium should be given if approved by your veterinarian.

More than one dog, or dog and puppy can be fed together but adults should be either tied or kept in separate rooms until they are adjusted to one another. Bowls for food must be kept widely apart, since jealousy over food is one of the most competitive of dog areas. One will always finish his dinner faster than the other and will usually charge over to the remaining bowl to finish that too, with an ensuing fight erupting.

With young puppies, even in the same litter, care must be taken that one does not gobble up most of the food, and the others have too little and end up underweight.

Both dogs and puppies should be left absolutely alone when eating. Teasing by children or others over food will lead to growling and snapping behavior which will be difficult to control later.

Food should be picked up after about 25 minutes, and unused portions refrigerated for a day. Never feed either hot food or cold food to dogs, but allow it to thaw or cool to room temperature.

If your dogs are eating well, snacks can be added in the form of dog biscuits. These are good for the teeth and dogs enjoy chewing them. No sweets, no fried foods, no high seasoning, and no bones should ever be given except beef leg bones which have been cooked. If your dogs are not eating well, eliminate snacks for a day.

If you have a new puppy and an adult dog, the pup will be getting additional meals. Feed your adult dog a snack when the pup is fed to avoid jealousy, or feed the pup in a separate room.

Adopted stray dogs may need special nutritional supplements to build them up. Consult your veterinarian.

Fussy eaters often respond to having another dog present at meals by eating better and faster . However, if he does not finish a meal do not let the other dog finish it or you will have an overweight problem with the second dog.

Dishes for food and water must be cleaned daily. Water should be fresh inside and outside the house, with the exception that, if you are having trouble housebreaking a pet, you may want to restrict his water after about 5:00pm unless he can go out to the yard at any time he wishes.

Good quality food in the right amounts will keep your dogs in tip top form, healthy and happy.

HEALTH AND FIRST AID

Dogs that are healthy have a bright and alert look. Their eyes shine and are not runny, the nose is damp, the gums pinkish, the teeth white and without stains and tartar, the coat has a shine, and the skin is free of problems.

Normal temperature for a puppy is 102°-103°, and for a dog is 101°-102°.

To enjoy your pets fully, they must be kept healthy physically and mentally. Mental fitness can most easily be seen in a happy attitude and an energetic, but not hyperactive demeanor.

The maintaince of a healthy dog means attention to several different areas. Dogs need:

- .a correctly balanced, high quality diet.
- .lots of water which is clean and fresh.
- .daily exercise.
- .frequent grooming, at least twice a week, and attention to any problems developing such as fleas and ticks, cuts on the feet, skin lesions or other problems.
- .a bath when the skin is dirty or the pup smells doggy.
- .the maintaince of a clean environment, which includes yard and bedding. A yard inspection every morning should include removal of dead mice, frogs, or birds. Tools and all toxic materials should be under lock and key. Lids on garbage cans should be tightly closed.
- .a dry and comfortable place to stay outside and inside, if they are kept both places. Dampness or chill will not only make the dog miserable, it will also lower the dogs resistance to disease.
- .during the teething period until 10-12 months of age, the dog will require chewing materials.

In checking over your dogs daily, any change should be mentally noted and evaluated. If one of your dogs seems sick, do not let him mix with others until the problem clears up. If his symptoms persist or are severe, take him to a veterinarian immediately.

Changes in dogs which should be noted include:

- bleeding, cuts or abrasions.
- vomiting, especially when combined with a temperature.
- convulsions.
- refusing food for more than 24 hours in adult dogs, or more than one meal in puppies.
- runny eyes or nose.
- coughing.
- tired, apathetic, listless.
- dull coat, dry skin, flaking condition.
- skin sores.
- hair falls out.
- excessive vomiting of yellow bile. Try allowing him to eat grass or milkbone.
- over heating, usually when confined to a car or truck in heat. Try spraying with cool water from hose to lower temperature.
- detection of worms in the feces. Other symptoms may be diarrhea, vomiting, loss of appetite or ravenous appetite, bloody stool.
- diarrhea. It can be caused by worms, stomach upset, start of disease, diet, or an allergy to a food or to milk. Try to determine the cause and correct condition immediately.

In case of accident be wary. If your dog is in pain he may try to bite you if you try to move him. Know how to tie the jaw shut by using gauze bandage tied several times around the jaw and then behind the ears. Move dog on a blanket if injured. Keep all other dogs away and transport to your veterinarian. Be sure medicine and anesthesia smells fade before reintroducing pet to dog pack. Strange smells may provoke an attack since they would not recognize pet.

The Dog Medicine Cabinet should include:

hydrogen peroxide, as disinfectant for cuts and to
   use on rough cloth to clean dog teeth
Milk of Magnesia, laxative for constipation. Dose
   1 teaspoon for small dog, 1 tablespoon for large.
Pepto-Bismol, for diarrhea
Epson Salts, to reduce swelling
rectal thermometer, to take temperature
Boric Acid solution, as an eye wash
aspirin, to lower high temperature, reduce inflama-
   tion or quiet a nervous dog
Sulfodene, to help heal skin problems, cuts
Ear-Rite, effective in mite problems, wax removal
mineral oil, for use in swabing outer ear clean
flea and tick prevention aids
worming medication, preferably prescribed by your
   veterinarian

If your dog has no physical symptoms but is unlike his usual self, he may be depressed, lonely, or bored. This means something is wrong with your schedule of care for the dogs. In serious cases dogs will lick their paws and fur excessively, bite their skin, be either listless or hyperactive and nervous, chewing everything in sight. A dog may appear to be defensive or even paranoid.

Such dogs need a new activity schedule, and greatly increased daily exercise. They need new experiences in their lives. If you cannot meet these needs due to time constraints, get assistance. Walk them on a rotating basis if necessary, play with and talk to them daily, give them more time in the exercise area with new toys and other dogs, and try to take one or more with you when you go out in the car. Bringing them into the house in shifts , one at a time, will also work wonders. A greatly enriched schedule must be followed to restore emotional or mental balance.

If you have done everything possible, and a dog still exhibits depression symptoms, consult your vet or an animal psycologist for evaluation.

When you first decide to add a dog to your home pack, try to find out all you can about him before bringing him home. Has he had shots and worming? What has he been eating? If he comes with a clean bill of health, it is not necessary to rush him to a veterinarian. If you cannot find out about him , keep him apart from your other dogs and have him checked by a vet immediately.

Prevention of injury and illness will go far toward keeping your pack healthy and happy, thus increasing your own pleasure in owning them.

FIRST DAY AND NIGHT WITH NEWCOMER DOG

If you have a choice, always try to bring in a new dog to your home at the beginning of a weekend, so you will have maximum time to orient the dog to his new surroundings and his new schedule, and to supervise his behavior, as well as to give time and attention to your resident dog or dog pack.

To avoid jealousy becoming intense, be sure you devote the usual time and attention to these old dog friends. It is worth this extra effort to try to keep them all happy in the beginning.

Allow the newcomer dog to become thoroughly familiar with the outside and inside of the house. His bed, bowls for food and water, leash and collar, and toys should all be ready for him.

As you lead him through his daily schedule, he will know when he can exercise, when he eats, and when and how he can eliminate.

Unless you are absolutely sure of the friendliness of your resident dog or pack, keep the newcomer entirely separate the first day. Everything is new to him and he should orient himself slowly. This is true also of other people and children in the household. They should meet the new dog for a few minutes at a time only. Don't overwhelm him with either people or dogs, especially if the dogs are hostile. He may run away or make a poor adjustment.

The most difficult time you will have with the newcomer dog will be the first night. Depending on his age, puppy or adult, he should be sleeping within earshot of the owner. Crying can be helped by offering some warm milk, wrapping a ticking clock in the puppy bed, or otherwise comforting the new pet, without giving too much sympathy.

In the ensuing days the most important tasks will begin i.e. analysis of the needs of the newcomer dog, and engineering his adjustment with the other resident dogs in your home.

NEEDS OF NEWCOMER DOGS

When you first acquire a new dog, consciously or unconsciously you are analyzing his needs and behavorial characteristics and trying to see how they can best be modified to fit into your home.

Assessment of needs of adult dogs is the more complex of course. Little puppies do not have the experiences in their lives which cause problems, in most cases.

Among the areas which you should note are:

housebreaking failures, inability to eliminate when walking on a leash outside the yard or in yard.

aggressiveness toward you and when it occurs, includes growling, snapping, threatening looks or behavior. This can occur when he eats, when you correct him verbally, when you take something from him he has taken and should not have etc.

knowledge of basic commands or failure to obey if he doesn't want to do so.

degree of friendliness toward other members of the immediate family, strangers who come to gate, people encountered when out walking on leash, other dogs, cats.

shy, nervous responses such as wetting when you first get home and greet him at the door, excessive barking, trembling, cringing, fear of being alone for a short time, fear of loud noises such as thunder.

degree of energetic behavior and when it occurs.

destructive behavior, chewing everything in sight, tearing paper, stealing things and chewing them up.

rough play with you, tendency to be excitable or rambunctious and hard to control.

problems involved with eating, such as eating the excrement of other dogs. This problem can often be cleared up by worming, if necessary, checking the diet for vitamin-mineral balances, and verbal corrections.

excessive barking for no known reason.

running away at every opportunity.

running after cars, joggers, bicycles, children.

Your knowledge of the specific needs of the newcomer dog are in addition to his general needs for good care in a routine schedule. Adjustments should be made which help correct his problems in the easiest way possible so trauma is minimized. Corrections should be consistent.
Since many different behavorial problems in dogs are due to inadequate exercise, boredom, and depression, the most important thing to do immediately is to get him on a good and active schedule, filled with things to do that will keep him too busy to get into mischief.

In general shy, fearful dogs need personal attention, love, and more gentle correction. Never harsh correction.

Dogs who fear people need to be socialized gradually.

Strong, aggressive dogs need a combination of discipline given in a fair way, and affection and praise for good behavior.

Dogs who are too competitive...won't let you take things from him or are too rambunctious and demanding and insist on having things their own way, must learn that what you want him to do comes first. You must always win in a contest of wills with your dog. Training is important with this dog and play should not be too rough or aggressive in type, such as tag or tug-of-war.

If you have begun to establish a good relationship and a bonding with your newcomer dog, he will try to please you. However, he will need time to get used to new behavorial patterns. He will make mistakes, forget, get stubborn or defensive, and tired and irritable, seeming to take two steps forward and one step backward. Be patient and love him.

At the same time, don't neglect your resident dogs. It will not only make them resentful and jealous of the new dog, but will create other problems as well. This important point bears repetition.

Every dog you own must have a special close relationship with you, a bonding that does not lessen regardless of whether you may acquire another dog. Spending time with him daily is an important aspect of this relationship. Don't reject him, take him for fewer walks or rides in the car. Treat all dogs as equally as possible. A dog who is rejected when it bids for your attention will stop making overtures and will become emotionally isolated and depressed. Make an effort to revitalize your relationships with all your dogs, again through an active schedule, new toys, and personal attention.

The care that puppies get before they come home with the new owner is very important to their behavioral patterns and adjustment capacity. Puppies that are traumatized by inadequate care, food, water, long trips, noise or other negative environmental conditions will experience negative effects.

If they have had little or no contact with humans they will tend to be unresponsive and hard to train. They will relate more to other dogs than to the owner. Or if the contact they have had has been negative for them, they may react aggressively toward people.

Lack of experiences outside their immediate kennel facility inhibits their natural curiosity and developmental learning ability, making them afraid.

Such puppies need lots of tender loving care. Again, an assessment of how they react to specific sets of circumstances must be noted and very gentle corrections begun. They may grow out of many problems, and will have to be trained out of others.

Older puppies in particular, need behavorial evaluation, after information has been gathered about their history and background.

The puppy must learn that you, the new owner, is fair and can be trusted. He must know that you will be good to him, and that his basic needs will be met daily, that you will protect him. In short, he must think of you as the greatest owner in the world.

The importance of the basic schedule for your dogs care cannot be stressed enough .

Some additional thoughts on the basic schedule follow.

SCHEDULE

When deciding on a dog schedule, it is important to try and put yourself mentally in the place of the dog. If you have one dog and work during the day, he is alone all day with nothing to do but sleep and chew a rawhide strip or play ball with himself. He looks forward with great excitment to your return home. You exercise him, feed him, and if he is lucky, spend the evening hours with him. Then he is expected to sleep again.

Day after day of this isolated routine makes him frantic and he frequently gets into trouble by doing things he should not. He gradually gets more and more aggressive, since he is usually not socialized during the day. He is not well adjusted.

You give him good food and love, but this is not enough to make him into the kind of dog you want him to be. Only you can do that, and it takes time and attention.

In my opinion, having more than one dog helps a great deal with the problem of loneliness and boredom, but it does create its own kind of problems.

You must be prepared to make a commitment to expend more time, energy, patience, and money to care for more than one. Many small adjustments will need to be made often to accomodate shifting circumstances and dog developmental needs. To determine what adjustments need to be made you need to spend time with your pets on a daily basis.

A schedule for a dog will help keep him free of
anxiety and lower stress by keeping his world
orderly. A few rules of daily behavior will set
limits for him. A balanced diet, and a dry and
warm place to sleep will help keep him healthy.
An owner who is both a leader and a pal will provide love and protection for him. And, now that
you will have another dog, he also has doggy
friends and perhaps a mate.

A good schedule for a dog includes on a daily basis:

walks in the yard for elimination purposes, as
    soon as he wakes up and again after his breakfast
    or before you go off to work, at noon , after
    you return from work, after dinner, at about
    7:30 pm, and just before you go to sleep.

Much depends on your facilities for the dog,
whether they are inside or outside in a fenced
yard or run, or include both inside and outside
through a dog port cut into your kitchen door.

exercise is a very important element. This is not
    simply allowing your dog to go into the yard. He
    will tend to stand there, waiting for you or
    for something to happen. Exercise is active running
    and jumping for at least one hour a day.

play in the yard in a more relaxed manner is import-
    ant. Play with another dog is excellent, or play
    with you with a ball or other toys.

a walk outside the yard with you on the leash will
    help to socialize him, since it gets him out of
    his immediate environment and into contact with
    new things, smells, and people.

rides in the car to the shopping mall, park, or to
    the beach where you may be able to let him go
    free without risk is an excellent change.

daily grooming, brushing and checking for physical problems, fleas, cuts, need for ear cleaning with a mineral oil dipped cotton ball, need for teeth cleaning with rough cloth dipped in hydrogen peroxide, and need for nails to be trimmed.

training time in basic commands, advanced work, or tricks can be enjoyable for the dog and make him more manageable.

All of these elements will give your dog variety and take care of his needs at the same time.

I have personally found that a long run early in the morning for about forty-five minutes is well worth the effort it takes me to get myself up and get going outside. The dogs have a chance to eliminate, as well as to get rid of some of that boundless energy that has built up overnight.

A well exercised dog early in the morning is quieter during the day, more relaxed, and will look for less mischief and be less irritable. On the other hand, a dog who waits all day for his major exercise until evening hours may well be frustrated, impatient, and full of energy all day, with greater potential for trashing your house, apartment, or yard, and generally acting in a naughty manner.

As I have suggested early in this book, once your schedule for your dogs has been worked out satisfactorily, vary it within the time frame for the sake of variety. Keep it interesting.

The same idea should be developed for all dog activities, individual or pack. If play with your dogs consists solely of throwing a ball, vary it with other equipment such as jumps. or teach a variety of tricks. You will have more fun and so will they.

More than one dog can participate in any schedule
you design as long as they can be controlled. A
long walk can be taken on a leash with two or even
more dogs, as dog walkers do. Multiple dogs can
run loose in isolated areas as long as they can be
controlled by group commands to "come", "go car"
or others. An adult dog and a puppy can go for
short walks together at a park or around your
property.

It is wise however, never to let your pets free near
a highway, since they will frequently chase things ,
real or imagined , and get hurt.

The key to a good schedule is to keep it well balanced with things needed to keep the dog healthy
mentally and physically. Two adult dogs may get a
good deal of exercise in the yard playing freely,
however if they are left without socializing walks
and contact with the owner, the pack behavior will
become more intense. They will fight more and
relate to you and the family less.

Dogs who get time and attention but are still in-
adequately socialized outside the immediate family,
will also tend to become more aggressive with
strangers, but less pack oriented.

If you want friendly dogs, choose a friendly puppy,
then continue a socialization program of activities
for it daily with both people and dogs. Take him
with you whenever possible, into different situations
and activities.

Your schedule for your dogs should then meet basic
dog needs, meet special needs of the individual dogs
and their problems, and be designed to gently shape
the dogs into the kind of dogs you want them to be.
In general, a good balance is the most satisfactory.

35

A Protective Mom and One of her Pups

Running Free in a Fenced-in Yard

Tied for a short time in the Shade with lots of Space

EXERCISE AND PLAY

All dogs need exercise every day. Although some require a little less than others, all dogs need exercise and play every day.

Although toy breeds can race around the house and get their muscles exercised, this does little to refresh them mentally or to alleviate their boredom. This serious problem of boredom is the core of behavorial problems of all kinds since dogs kept as pets have little or no work to do daily. Misdirected energy is frequently destructive energy. Housebound dogs can be self-destructive.

Larger breeds, of course, require much more exercise.

The need for sufficient exercise is a basic requirement of dogs and cannot be ignored without making the pet neurotic to a degree.

Many people are familiar with the term "cabin fever", which is a feeling of being cooped-up with the walls closing in on you when confined to the house for several days or weeks due to illness or a bad winter storm. Inside exercise may help to an extent, but somehow we all need to get out of our immediate environment and "get fresh air". It may be even more important to animals.

Dogs need exercise and play every day, regardless of the weather. It will keep their bowel movements regular, they will eat better, and be better balanced mentally. Puppies in particular need to develop their muscles and their coordination, work off stress and tensions, and just have fun. If they are dried off with towels when they return, there should be no ill effects.

Obeying the Command "Down" but he doesn't Like it

Sitting Quietly in a Car

Exercise and Fun Playing with Another Dog in Yard

Although they may not be housebound, dogs kept tied in yards do not fare any better. After a few days of being kept tied to the side of a house, any dog will become more aggressive and frantic, and more fearful and paranoid, usually accompanied by constant whining and almost continual barking.

There is a family in my immediate neighborhood who keeps their dog tied in just such a way. The owner refuses to change to a more humane method of treatment, although several people have spoken to him about it. Although he takes it to the park for about 45 minutes several times a week, it is returned to the same line upon return. It is not walked again, not spoken to by the family, and is generally ignored , having neither dog or human pals.

This unfortunate creature barks. When he barks the owner has been seen to beat it with a golf club or throw rocks at it. Then, having made the dog neurotic, he calls the dog "crazy." This man's dogs frequently bite him, and those bites I am sure, contain all the resentment the dog has built up for the owner since puppyhood.

The toll on dogs who are thus mistreated through neglect cannot be calculated. And, at the same time, the owner is deprived of the kind of rewarding relationship with a family pet a dog owner is usually seeking.

Fenced-in yards or exercise areas where dogs can run and play by themselves help a great deal, especially for the more relaxed play aspect of exercise.

Adult dogs who can barely tolerate one another can sometimes be made friendlier by sharing play activity, either in a neutral area or in their own yard.

Play recently solved a dog problem for me personally. My older female dog refused to accept a male puppy I had acquired. Her threats to jump on the pup and bite him forced us to keep them separated. After two months of various efforts on our part, the situation had not changed.

One day, I secured the older dog for a short time to a tree, while playing with the puppy in the yard with a ball, running and having lots of fun. For the first time she showed jealousy of our fun, and wanted to play too. Keeping her on the line, I let the pup advance with the ball, and she made her first playful movement by raising her rump and wagging her tail. When he jumped at her in play, she growled again, but, the ice had been broken. They were on the way to becoming the good friends that they are today.

Just as exercise has assumed increased importance in the health of people in the last decade, I would like to reinforce its importance in the lives of dogs. It comes close to being a panacea for many problems and, together with other aspects of good care, is basic.

Walking dogs outside your yard to socialize them is also important. Each dog must be leash trained to walk quietly at your left side, and not lunge ahead when provoked by a cat, dog, child, or car. Walking more than one dog on separate leashes depends on the behavior of the dogs. They may try to play with one another, one may try to dash off, they may both try to dash off in different directions at the same time, or they may run around you in a circle getting the leashes tangled in your legs.

For the best results, dogs should be about the same size so gait is similiar. Each should walk well on a leash separately. For two well behaved dogs, a tandem chain can be used with one leash.

Having stressed the importance of exercise, a word must be said about not over-exercising them. This can occur today when dogs run with their jogger owners longer than they should, or more frequently than they should. Also dogs should never be run in the heat of day. If you jog, take your pet in the cool of the day or leave him home and exercise him later. Common sense should always be used regarding pets. Do not neglect to check the pads of the feet after each exercise period.

Although the needs of the dog are an individual matter, to be determined by his breed, age, and physical condition, this basic need is present in all dogs. Even dogs who are lazy and need active encouragement to exercise, suffer ill effects if they do not receive sufficient exercise. This is a vital element in your schedule of dog care.

HOUSEBREAKING

Housebreaking is another area that must be done individually. Dogs of the same age and size will usually still have their own physical rythmn and will need to go out to eliminate at different times.

Housebreaking problems can be greatly lessened if the dog or puppy you acquire has come from a clean kennel which promptly cleans up runs. Dogs from a doubtful environment will take longer to learn what it is you want them to do.

The easiest and least traumatizing way to deal with housebreaking is to take the puppy or dog outside of the house to the yard on supervised walks every 2-3 hours depending on age.

Puppies under four months have little physical control and must be taken out every two hours and also after each meal, after each nap, and before you go to sleep.

These frequent walks to the yard are easy and pleasant, and your puppy or dog will soon get the idea of eliminating in the grass, or at the curb in the city, especially if you have other dogs that use that same vicinity.

A puppy or dog that is not housebroken must be confined to a special area inside the house, which has paper spread on the floor, unless you carefully supervise where he is going and what he is doing, in addition to his walks outside.

Punishment for a mistake should be limited to a severe verbal "no, no", and the dog walked outside immediately. If he eliminates in the proper place, he should be praised each time with "good boy".

I do not favor crate training for housebreaking since locking a dog in a crate at night can cause stress and possible physical discomfort.

Taking the dog out until he gets the idea of eliminating outside is the least traumatizing of the housebreaking methods. Combined with paper training as an alternative when you cannot take him out, these two methods are recommended.

RIDING IN A CAR

Another area for individual dog evaluation is whether this dog has had experience riding in a car and whether he is calm during the ride. To find this out, open the car windows a bit for fresh air and take your newcomer dog for a five minute ride before he has a meal, rather than after he eats.

Taking several dogs out together in the back of the family station wagon for a short trip to the park, the beach, or the supermarket, will help socialize them to the outside world even if they do not always get out of the vehicle to sniff and run.

If you do let them out of the car in a secluded spot, be sure it is off the highway. Even if you have the dog on a leash, he may lunge if frightened and be injured.

To ride in a car with several dogs, each must be trained to ride individually, then trained to ride quietly with one other dog, and then with more of them if there is sufficient space.

Good judgement is always necessary with your individual dogs. Don't make your rides too long. Never put dogs that do not get along well together in a car, since the ride will not stop them from fighting.

To avoid danger to the driver, dogs should be restrained in some way from jumping into the front from the back of the car. Today, there are mesh barriers that can be obtained for installation between the drivers seat and the rear of the station wagon.

Lacking a mesh barrier, one dog can be tied to each car door handle with his leash, leaving room for him to move a bit but not to jump.

The idea is to keep the dog from jumping, from nibbling on your hair or ear, or slobbering on your neck while you are driving.

Thoroughly trained dogs can, of course, be loose.

In semi-rural areas, some owners ride around with
multiple dogs in the back of pick-up trucks. This
can be a dangerous and abusive practice.

Dogs will jump out of trucks at red lights into
the middle of heavy traffic. They will jump out to
chase something they see. They will sometimes fall
out when the truck swings around a curve.

Truck beds get hot and uncomfortable in summer heat,
and wet and cold in rainy or frigid weather. Dogs
get sick easily from temperature extremes and dampness. Cinders and dust from winds can infect their
eyes and ears.

If a truck is your only means of dog transport,
extreme care must be taken. Tie-in the dogs so
they cannot jump out , and be constantly aware of
the weather conditions...heat, rain, and cold.
Drive carefully, without wild swings which throw
dogs off their feet or out of trucks. Keep out
of traffic jams, and take them out early in the
cool of the morning or evening if possible.

GROOMING

Much of the material you need to know about grooming
has already been given. However it should be noted
that grooming is an individual matter. Different
dogs have different coats, different skin problems,
and are of different ages. Any selection of pro-
ducts to treat your dogs should be individually
decided.

For example, be extremely careful using flea pre-
parations with puppies. Use only according to
labels.

I have found flea collars to be unsatisfactory for
multiple dogs, since they play together and will

frequently be found pulling at another dogs collar with their teeth, thus ingesting this hazardous material. Flea shampoos, powers, and sprays are better for a pack.

Ears, teeth, and nails must all be checked, and changes in the eyes noted which may entail a visit to your veterinarian, such as cataract conditions.

Gentle but thorough brushing will do a great deal of good, loosening dead skin, stimulating oil glands, and getting rid of dirt and debris. Give a bath to your dogs when the skin itself is dirty.

For bathing, use warm water, a good flea shampoo, and dry completely with towels, whether bathed inside or outside. Be sure you have rinsed well. If a dryer is used, test temperature on your own skin first. Fluff up the hair to dry it, and then brush lightly when dry.

MULTIDOG ADJUSTMENT

MULTIDOG ADJUSTMENT

One of the most difficult problems you will have potentially when bringing in a new dog to your home is the problem of adjustment of the newcomer dog to your resident dogs and to the immediate family. It can be very easy or very difficult.

Dog owners are often surprised when their previously well adjusted dog becomes unreasonably jealous of the puppy or newcomer dog. Owner behavior is very important in this situation. Your resident dog is waiting to see how your behavior and the behavior of others in the house will change toward him. Keep in mind that his place must not be taken over by the newcomer if you want them to adjust well. Give him as much attention as before and try and treat all dogs equally.

Each combination of dogs and puppies have their own special problems, just as they have their own personalities and life experiences. Your goal in adjustment is to have them adjust to living together, which means sharing their territory, their things, and their human owners. The ages, sex, breeds, temprement, and life experiences to date, and current environmental factors all play a role in their behavior patterns with one another.

A dog who has been emotionally dependent on one or more other dogs will tend to be friendlier, re - gardless of sex or territory. If there has been a death of one of their dog friends in your family and the remaining dogs miss him, this is especially true. Not always however, since jealousy may outweigh this need.

The best adjustment is frequently made between a mature male and a mature female who has had puppies. They will get along best because of sex interest.

A mature resident female will often fight both males and females and seem to adjust more slowly to their presence, seemingly more jealous .

Females with puppies with her will fight all dogs viciously, protecting her pups and also any en - crouchment on the territory where she hopes to bring up her young. She also may be more defensive than usual with the immediate family and with strangers who come to the house.

The most vicious fighters are the mature males. If they are aggressive they may fight over any intrusian on their territory, for supremacy over one another, for the favor of a female, and for certain favorite places in the environment such as a certain place to sleep.

After accessing your situation with respect to your newcomer dog as an individual,and your resident dogs and their typical behavior, move slowly toward adjustment.

NEVER FORCE THEM TO SOCIALIZE if there is obvious hostility, such as growling or snapping. Give them as much time as it takes to adjust from a safe distance.

Remember, any newcomer dog has much to adjust to in his new and strange environment. He must learn about you and your expectations, his new schedule, his immediate environment, the food, the other people in the house, and other things that may be strange for him. He is probably feeling tense and stressed to some extent from the immediate adjustment problems.

To help in adjustment, introduce the newcomer to one other dog or one person at a time. Sit dogs close to one another on leash, but not close enough to bite. Keep them there for 5-15 minutes, or as long as one hour if they are quiet. However, if there is straining at the leash, barking, and snarling, remove them from the same vicinity and try again another day.

Most dogs are calmer in the afternoon and more energetic and excitable in the morning and evening. Try adjustment in the afternoon.

Feed them together, again tied so they cannot charge at one another. Separate their bowls of food. Feed them the same food, except for a puppy and a grown dog who require different diets.

The basic idea in putting them near one another is to get them accustomed to having the other dog as a part of their environment and not a stranger intruding into the area. This helps adjustment.

Play as a lever to break through the hostility has been described in the previous chapter. It can be very helpful with normally playful dogs.

Two stable dogs of the same size can be turned loose in the yard or exercise enclosure with muzzels. They will quickly determine who is most dominant and will adjust quickly after that.

However, never expect a puppy to make an adjustment with a grown dog in this way. Young puppies left alone with older dogs run the risk of being killed through biting and shaking at the neck. Even if the adult dog is muzzeled, he will pounce on the pup causing massive internal injuries and breaking bones, since the pup is seen as a prey object or an object of jealousy.

Puppies need to sometimes grow larger, nearer the size of the adult dog, and develop sexual characteristics before an adult dog will consider them as dogs worthy of their good will.

It is important to emphasize that if you try to force adjustment between two dogs, you are running the risk of injury to or death of a puppy, and also injury to two adult dogs.

Continued hostility between two adult dogs, if allowed to intensify over several encounters due to your eagerness to "get them together" may result in such deep seated hatred that those two dogs will never be friends.

To help reassure the resident dogs that nothing will change because there is a newcomer dog now, treat them all equally and do the same things with them you have always done. Giving the resident dogs their things first will help. Talk to them together. Sit with them for a moment outside together. Pat each. Let them exercise with you once a day...first one then the other. By treating them equally you are establishing their expectations, and by giving things to the resident dogs first you are reassuring them that you recognize their status with you.

Never leave a newcomer dog with other dogs at night unless you are absolutely certain adjustment has been completed. Often dogs who appear adjusted are merely tolerating the other dog because they know the owner wants them to do so. In such superficial relationships , dogs have been known to gang-up on a newcomer and kill him when the owner is absent, such as at night.

Also, do not house a newcomer dog next to an antagonistic dog in a kennel run, since they will attempt to fight through the fence and will sustain damage to teeth and feet.

If you have tried all of the above techniques and nothing works, try to get adjustment by putting the newcomer in a boarding kennel overnight. Inevitably the resident dog will look for him and may be happier to see him when he returns the next day. Don't leave him away longer than this however, or the resident dog will think he has gotten "rid of"the dog , and will still be upset when he shows up with you again.

You could try bringing in a third dog from the neighborhood who is friendly, to provide a new balance to the group. However, this dog must be really friendly, or they may all gang up on the newcomer.

If however, you find yourself in a situation with two stubborn and hostile dogs who show no sign of compromise, you will have to keep them permanently separated, or get rid of one of the dogs. Multidog back yard breeders sometimes have two distinct packs or small groups of dogs who get along well together but cannot be mixed with the other pack. It is worth it for breeding purposes, and the extra care and facilities necessary can be provided. This is up to you to decide.

AFTER ADJUSTMENT

Assuming that the dog you have brought into the

pack is now adjusted, the following is suggested:

- do not put a pack of dogs in your back yard and assume that because they play together they will be well adjusted. They need that well rounded schedule often mentioned in this book. A dog must have a sense of individuality...a sense of self ...and a sense of his relationship to you. If left with a pack, he will be dominated by what the leader of the pack wants and what the pack does, and will not be a good pet for a family or individual.

Stick with your dog schedule and separate your dogs for various activities throughout the day, inside and outside the house, in the car, for a walk outside the yard, and in individual play with you. Each dog should also have time alone for short periods.

- two or more puppies of the same age, brought into the house together can experience this same kind of problem. It is easy to keep them together to play, eat, and sleep, but it is not good for their individual development. One pup will tend to dominate the other and they will both experience dependency problems.

A sense of individual identity must be fostered. If this is not done, the dominant one will become stubborn and harder to train and the submissive one will become shy, nervous, and anxious.

In extreme dependency relationships, when one dog dies the remaining pet may refuse to eat and will actually pine away.

To avoid such dependency, train dogs separately, play with them alone, take them out one at a time occasionally, minimize stress, and have a strong relationship yourself with each dog.

- even though your dogs appear adjusted fighting may break out in the pack or when you are walking one or more dogs outside the yard on leash. If you are in the yard, spray water on the dogs from the hose, give them commands, and try pulling their tails or hind legs. This works best if two people are pulling at the same time.

  Never pull their collars, since they may bite you.

  If the fight is with a strange dog, be aware of the hostility before it starts. Don't try to make friends with the dog, yell at it to "get home" and have a rock ready to throw, back slowly away with your dog on leash, and avoid staring him straight in the eye.

  If the strange dog lunges at you and your dog, drop the leash and fold your arms across your face and head, kick at the dog and yell in a commanding tone of voice. Wash and disinfect any wounds and report the incident to the Department of Health. A tetanus shot may be advisable. Your dog should be wearing a license and an identification tag in case he runs away after an encounter of this type and gets lost.

GAMES DOGS PLAY WITH OWNERS

Almost all dog games with owners are competitive in nature and are related to aggression and a try for dominance in some way. A few of these games are:

- "she's my mother not your mother". This game is most often played when you are out walking with several of your dogs and they are running free. One will run up quickly when you call them and then try to keep others from coming up to you also by facing them and chasing them back away from you.

- "I want to be your favorite dog". This game is played, often by the newcomer dog, who makes a great effort to do everything better and quicker then the others in the pack when they are all together. He makes it obvious that he wants to be your favorite dog and be the center of your attention.

- "you can't have it, even if I don't want it". This game is played with one other dog and some favorite old bone or toy, or bed inside the house. One dog ignores the item until another dog in the pack tries to take it, when it then becomes very valuable to the first dog.

- "you can't tell me what to do" or "I may be smarter than you are". This game is played by an aggressive and dominant dog trying to get his own way with you and/or members of the immediate family. He will deliberately disobey or act in a jealous way with a husband or wife of the owner. Firm control is necessary, combined with love and patience. Each person must establish their own relationship with the dog, but all must go by the same rules.

- "you left me for the weekend and I don't know who you are any more". This game can be played by any number of dogs who are left with another family member while the owner, for whom they wait, does not appear for several days or longer. There may be no joyous welcome upon his return, He may be totally ignored.

How does your pack relate to you? What are they trying to tell you? How can you adjust their schedule so things will work better for all concerned?

CAT AND DOG ADJUSTMENT

Another factor that must be taken into consideration in bringing in a new puppy or dog is the resident cat, if you have one or more.

This can be a serious problem also if you have a mature cat who has been raised with your resident dog. Cats will also defend their territory and are jealous of intrusions.

They will attack a new puppy in their yard without hesitation, and will sometimes stand their ground when confronted by a grown dog, ready to scratch at the eyes.

Mother cats with kittens are especially aggressive, for the same reason that all mothers in the animal kingdom seem to be, defense of the young and their territory.

On the other hand, if the dog you bring in has also been raised with a cat and is not aggressive toward them, they will work out a relationship in time. Expose them to one another for short periods only in the beginning and observe their behavior closely.

A simpler solution would be to keep cat and dog facilities separate.

CHILDREN AND MULTIPLE DOGS

Many children instinctively love dogs and want one for themselves. This may be one of the reasons for bringing in a new pup or young adult dog to the household. Such a child can assume some of the responsibility for a new pet, but the ultimate responsibility must lie with the adults.

Rules must be established for children in the family in their relations with a single dog or with multiple dogs. These rules should include:

- when they can play with the dogs and when they must leave them alone to sleep or eat.

- where they can play with dogs, singly or in a pack. Exercise yard only? Inside the house?

- how they can play with the dog. Gentle and protective relationships with puppies, how to walk dog on leash, how to pick up a dog, how to behave toward dog i.e. no teasing, pulling ears or tail.

- what their responsibilities are for the dogs.

- how to inform the adults in the family if anything seems wrong with a dog, such as a cut foot, loose stool, or listless behavior.

Since you are adding a dog, the children you may have in your family already have dog rules of behavior. Perhaps it is time these were refreshed and/or revised to do things a better way. If the new dog is a different breed and age this may be important.

Potential problems of your children with multiple dogs are not great if the child has had a good relationship with the resident dog, unless you are bringing in a dog with aggression problems. Usually a good caring relationship can be extended easily to include the new dog.

Initial supervision is important however to determine that there is no sign of jealousy of the new dog on the part of the child, and no aggression directed toward it. Including the children in your discussions about taking in another dog and then planning for it together will help gain acceptance for the pet.

To repeat, much depends on your individual situation and the nature of your dog pack. In general, rough play with dogs should be avoided by children and also by adults. Dogs are more aggressive in packs then when they are alone. No games should be played where the dogs chase the child, since they might knock a child down in excitment even if they do not bite. Prey instincts come into play in chasing games.

If a child becomes frightened when playing with a dog or dogs, the child should freeze and call for help from the adults in the family.

Never permit play between newcomer dogs and children if there is any sign of aggression on either side. Adult dogs, even those who are supposed to like children, have an unknown dimension involved in their responses toward your children. Monitor their behavior .

Restrictions for children should also be set up when your bitch has puppies. Mother dogs are naturally protective. She may not tolerate a child she has previously been friendly with and may growl protectively, thus possibly hurting the childs feelings and causing future problems in their relationship. Talk over this situation with your children in advance, not after the harm has been done. The general rule here is complete privacy for mother and pups for the first week, and only 5 minute visits of anyone but owner after that. Children must always be supervised and not allowed to touch puppies until they are older.

Babies must never be left alone with an adult dog. In this situation, the baby is the newcomer and the jealousy of the dog for territory and the owners affection will focus on the "intruder". Although most are entirely trustworthy and will even protect a human baby, it is better to make absolutely certain of the safety of the infant or toddler.

Another important rule regarding children is that neighborhood children should not be permitted to enter your yard and play with your dogs at any time. Even if your dogs are enclosed in runs or are tied in the yard, you cannot control the behavior of other children toward the dogs. Possible teasing can cause your dogs to become much more aggressive toward children and ruin their disposition.

The adjustment of a newcomer dog or puppy to another dog or a pack of dogs, and to other members of your family, is not a static problem. Situations will shift and change as people and animals develop or circumstances change in their lives. An awareness of changing needs of your dogs as individuals and as a pack is needed, with the goal of balance in their behavior and personalities .

SEX AND BREEDING

As with all animals, sexual development takes place from the time dogs are puppies. Curiosity about another puppy or dog, sniffing body parts, sniffing where another dog has eliminated and scratching and kicking the ground after their own elimination, are all connected to sexual development. Puppies will mount one another in play. These sexual manifestations are natural and should be ignored by owners.

Adult males, if frustrated, may jump on anything available in the area, including the leg of a person. If you do not want to mate your dog for some reason, consult with your veterinarian about neutering. Vigorous exercise every day will also help the behavior situation.

Males are sexually mature between one year and eighteen months. Usually they will start to lift their leg to urinate at about that time. Until then they urinate in a squat.

Females are sexually mature when they go into heat, usually between nine months and twelve months of age. However, although they are sexually mature, they are not physically fully developed and strong. For this reason, it is best to wait until the second heat to breed.

Not all dogs need to breed. Wild dog and wolf packs make natural selection choices and permit only the dominant bitch in the group to breed. This self-regulation holds down the pack population so that food is more adequate. Other females may or may not ever have puppies.

In civilization, owners of dogs have the option of breeding or not breeding. If there are puppies, the owner is the one responsible for them.

The sex drive is an important one. Dogs who live in a community where other dogs are breeding are certainly aware of it, and will feel frustrated if they are confined and not allowed to mate. However, bear in mind that you can take your dogs on special fun trips during stressful times to get them out of their immediate environment. Or, you can have them spayed or neutered.

Back-yard breeders usually have facilities for up to six dogs behind their houses and have puppies for sale occasionally. Such facilities are necessary for a variety of circumstances, none more important than when the owner expects to breed.

NOT BREEDING WHEN IN HEAT

Even if you occasionally breed your female , you may not want to breed every time she comes into season. Females should be bred every other heat for health reasons. Or perhaps you do not want to breed her at all and also do not want to have her spayed.

In these circumstances, separate facilities are very important to house her away from the other dogs. She can be exercised in an enclosed exercise yard alone, but must also be watched so she does not jump over the fence.

She can also be taken out in the car and exercised at some location away from home, where no other dogs are present. Male dogs can pick up a scent from some distance and will come running, so do not allow your female off leash from the 5th to the 21st day of the 21 day heat cycle.

An enclosed yard at home, and male dogs barking at any strange dog who may appear, will help keep most dogs away. However, it is best to take her out of the area for exercise and elimination most of the time. Normally obedient dogs behave strangely when in season, and both male and female will disobey and seek out a mate. Dog-tex belts and scent deodorizers can be helpful, but try to keep things as natural and possible so the dogs are not stressed unduly. Keep her in the house when not exercising.

Your male dogs will be much more likely to fight if a female is in season in the area. A strange male entering your property will fight with the resident males, and males within your household will fight for dominance...on the assumption that the winner will get the female. Don't permit fights!

BREEDING

Females are interested in active sex only during their heat periods, which occur every six months. The greatest chance of her becoming pregnant is between the 9th and the 13th days of the heat. It is generally thought that breeding during these days will result in more puppies than breeding at the beginning or the end of the cycle.

To breed profitably, purebred dogs should be mated with other purebred dogs, and their pedigree papers and registration papers must be available to buyers.

Although all this seems like a simple matter. It is really not. You cannot force dogs to breed. They must want to do it. Making friends in advance helps a great deal.

In one example I know, a young female German Shepard had her choice of several male German Shepards, but refused to breed. On the last day of her heat she escaped her yard to race up the hill and breed with a black Labrador Retriever who lived several houses away. One pup resulted...a large mixed breed male. The owner of this particular dog was very upset, since she had already tentatively "sold" several pups she thought she would have, and now would not have. Dogs have minds of their own when it somes to romance.

The best way I know to get around this problem is to let the potential suitors play and make friends with the female long before the heat period. No courtship or no contact before mating is not a satisfactory answer and probably will put off the male or the female , or both.

When in heat, bring the bitch to the male. The reasons for this are that the male may not perform as well off his home territory, and also so that he won't know how to get to the females home and thus not try to follow her there and perhaps be injured or killed by a car.

On the favored days in the heat cycle, the female should stand firm and will flag her tail to one side, indicating that she is ready to be bred. There is also a lightening of the discharge. During mating, dogs will become "tied" for 2-3 minutes or even longer. The breeding process is best carried out in privacy.

The bitch can stay with the male for an hour or two and should then be returned home. A return visit two days later is a good idea, and should be a part of the agreement for a stud fee, a puppy, or other.

Problems in mating are often caused by size differences. Mates should be selected who are nearly the same size.

A female who takes a strong fancy to a special dog often will not breed with another dog, regardless of what else you may do, but will mate with that dog willingly.

Shy females have often been frightened in some way by the mating process...perhaps a number of neighborhood dogs have forced their attentions on her and the owner has not protected her from the abuse and the ensuing fighting. She will refuse to mate.

Some dogs have no dog friends and are not socialized toward their own kind, preferring the company of humans. These dogs may not breed easily.

I do not favor restraint or forced mating practices because of the psychological cost to the female. There may or may not be a possibility in artificial insemination if all natural methods fail.

Mating is best when it is free and natural, with selected dogs who know and play together often. Breeding should be with one dog only, unless there is no mating.

HAVING PUPPIES

Whether planned or accidental, a mating usually results in puppies after a gestation period of 63 days. It is your responsibility to be sure those puppies are born strong and healthy, which starts with proper care of the mother before she gives birth. Consult with your veterinarian about her physical condition, diet, extra calcium and vitamins, and need for early worming.

The first indication of pregnancy will be a reddening of the teats. After that there will be abdominal enlargement, and an increase in appetite and body weight.

Exercise during this period should be curtailed and under no condition should she be ordered or trained to do anything violent, like jumping. Other than this precaution, frequent short walks are good for her health and will help in elimination. She is a good judge of what she can do.

A delivery area should be prepared in advance which is darkened, dry, secure, and of a comfortable temperature. A delivery box should be provided large enough for the mother to stretch out and also have lots of room for her puppies. She should be familiar with it before giving birth.

Pups will be born usually between five minutes to an hour apart. If pups are born further apart than this, watch carefully as the mother may be in trouble. Caesarean section is sometimes necessary when there is a lot of straining and no pup appears. Call your veterinarian if your female is in actual labor for hours without any resulting puppy.

During delivery the owner can assist the mother by easing the puppy out with a rough towel, taking care not to pull but just supporting the birth. If a puppy is turned, take one leg out first and ease the puppy out. In a normal birth by a young and healthy female, very little assistance will be needed.

After all the puppies are born the mother should appreciate some warm milk and a short walk outside. In a long labor, milk can be given during the birth.

Each puppy arrives in a membrane which will rupture. The mother will bite the umbilical cord and attempt to eat the afterbirth. You can remove them before she does so or not. If she does not lick the nose and mouth of the pup at birth, you must wipe them so it can breath. Be sure she does not roll over on a puppy as she shifts her weight around the box giving birth and nursing those that have been born. Puppies cannot move well when first born and will be unable to get out from under the mother if she becomes confused and one is caught beneath or behind her in the box.

Puppies eyes will remain closed for about ten days. Do not expose to sunlight for about a week after they are open.

The mother will continue to have a dark red discharge for some days after giving birth. If this discharge turns bright red or greenish, take her to the veterinarian. Some breeders are now routinely giving an injección of Pitocin to avoid infection of the uterus (metritis). Certainly in the case of infection this must be done.

The mother keeps the puppies clean and feeds them for about three weeks. After that they should be fed a little diluted evaporated milk and puppy food for part of their four meals. But do not remove them from the mother competely. Gradual weaning is best.

Keep the puppy place clean and dry by removing newspapers and replacing them a number of times a day. If pups learn a clean environment is best they will housebreak easier.

To get good homes for puppies, the socialization needs and developmental needs of the pups must be met.

Initially pups are aware of the mother.
At three weeks they are aware of their litter mates and begin to interact with them, playing, sniffing growling, and pouncing.

At four weeks puppies are aware of you as a person. It is good to spend five minutes twice a day with each pup individually to pet and play with him.

They should be taking short walks outside their immediate kennel. Their environment can be enriched with raw hide chews, balls, boxes to climb into, and other activity enhancers.

At seven weeks they can form attachments to people. For this reason it is good to sell them at seven or eight weeks of age. At this age they will also listen to simple commands, such as "no,no", and will sometimes obey.

Attention to the developmental and socialization needs of pups is critical to their personality development and the extent to which they will be friendly to people when they are shown.

As a responsible owner, remember to give the rest of your pack care and attention so jealousy does not develop. Keep them away from the mother and her puppies. She will guard them viciously. Keep other people away entirely for three days or a week when they are first born, with only short supervised visits after that time.

When selling puppies, screen the potential buyers carefully for facilities, time, and their attitude toward dogs, together with the type of care they normally would give a dog. Do not hesitate to deny a purchase of one of your puppies if the circumstances seem to be unsuitable for the happiness and well being of the dog.

TRAINING AND TRICKS

Training, corrections, and tricks are the ways you control your dogs, and also have fun with them. Packs of dogs cannot be controlled without individual training of each dog first. Therefore, as you acquire a new dog he should be trained as an individual, and the dogs you already have should not be allowed to forget what they already know.

It is important to remember that the basic purpose of training is to make your dogs happier and better pets and companions for you and your family, in addition to the need to control their actions.

Before giving attention to basic obedience, which is the core of training, a word should be said about the dog kept for protection purposes.

Most dogs will bark when a strange person or automobile approaches you or your property, since dogs are loyal and territorial about where they live. Some dogs are aggressive and must learn to be quiet when this command is given by the owner upon determining the purpose of the uproar. If they do not learn this lesson they may attack a stranger and bite. This instinctive guarding is sufficient for the protection purposes of most families and individuals.

If you need enhanced protection involving protection of property or attack on command work, do not attempt to train the dog yourself. Sharpening the dog to attack under specific circumstances can be dangerous for an untrained owner to do. Although protection dogs are never totally reliable, the best training can be given best by a professional trainer who knows protection and attack work thoroughly. However, for most individuals, this type of training should not be necessary or desirable under average family conditions.

From the day your new puppy or dog arrives at your home you are beginning to correct and train him in the way you want him to be. More serious training can begin from about the age of eight months and will continue until about eight years of age with success.

Basic training for each dog should cover obedience to the commands of:

sit, stay, come, heel, down, and the combination basic commands of sit-stay and down-stay.

Once all your dogs are adjusted to one another and know their basic commands they must also learn to obey group commands, such as "dogs sit" or "dogs go car" or importantly "dogs quiet". This eliminates the need to call each dog by name and giving the same order several times before the order is obeyed.

INDIVIDUAL DOG OBEDIENCE TRAINING

In training, as in your initial evaluation of the needs of your newcomer dog, his disposition is an important factor in how to approach the task. Before training starts you have presumably been working to modify undesirable characteristics and problems in behavior of the pet.

For example, if you want a good protection dog, you should not expect it from a nervous, shy, or very friendly dog. The former will turn and run under fire and the latter will welcome all comers to your door whether they are desirable or not.

I had a personal experience with this contrast in personality when, a number of years ago, I adopted a female pit bull. Contrary to their present aggressive image today, this five year old dog was the sweetest animal I have ever owned. She welcomed anyone who came with a wagging tail and what looked like a big grin, tongue hanging out one side of her mouth. My other dog at the time was a Collie-German Shephard mix. He would bark protectively at the same time she was wagging her tail, making quite a contrast to visitors and service people. I could not rely on the female to protect the house, although the potential is always there with the pit bull. But, I could take her anywhere and was always sure of her friendly attitude toward man or other dogs.

On the other hand, a vicious dog will never be entirely trustworthy or steady in his responses. If you bring in an aggressive dog, do not enhance his aggression by frustrating him in any but the most necessary ways, such as in training. Do not tie him up for longer than one hour and do not discipline him unfairly or nag him with a steady stream of confusing orders. Create a relaxed atmosphere for this dog and let him play naturally with the pack and give him plenty of exercise. His time with you will be especially important in gaining his trust, so that he does not react defensively and with aggression. Say "no, no" if he puts his teeth on you in any way and discourage aggression when it seems serious within the pack.

The best temprement for training is a quiet, steady, and moderately friendly dog, who is alert to what goes on around him and has a good attitude toward doing new things and toward obeying commands.

As a trainer, your own attitude while teaching the newcomer dog is very important. Your techniques vary.

The shy dog you have been trying to socialize and reassure must be gently handled. He must have confidence in you.

The slow, stubborn, or lazy dog must be energized by an enthusiastic trainer, who uses a "hurry up, this is fun" tone of voice.

The aggressive, strong minded dog needs quiet but firm handling, correction when required, praise when he does well, and enough activity to keep him alert and interested. Be fair but tough with him if needed.

The dog that plays and clowns when you are trying to train him must learn when he can play and when not. Praise him when he behaves seriously and don't laugh at him when he clowns at inappropriate times.

The suspicious dog mistrusts people and the environment in general. He needs to gain confidence in you before he will obey commands. Training must wait until you have established a good strong tie with him.

Although your attitude may vary with each dog, the basic ingredient is the need for the dog to have confidence in you and trust your intent and actions. Without rapport and bonding with each dog, training cannot be successful and will be filled with behavorial problems. Correct fairly and praise lavishly.

It is an accepted fact that dogs learn through associating their acts with pleasant or unpleasant results and with the commands of the trainer. In training, unpleasant results are those corrections that should be made with the leash and chain training collar.

At other times, using the gentlest correction that

works well is the rule that is best for all concerned.

Use of loud noise, such as throwing a tin can near the pet to get him to stop barking, or hitting the floor near the pet with a folded newspaper, can be effective. Pack barking can be stopped in this way.

Some owners now like isolation of a pet in a far off corner or kennel run for a short time as a correction, after which they will start fresh again. I am personally doubtful that the pet understands the connection between his act and the isolation. But what it may accomplish is getting the pet out of your way for awhile, even though it is useless as a correction. It also gives your pet time alone to calm down if needed.

Other corrections must be directed toward the problem, but always choose the kindest way. If your large Mastiff puppy jumps up on you, knocking you over, every time you arrive home or give him the "come" command, you must correct. Do this by raising your knee to the dogs chest rather than stepping on his toes or squeezing his front paws, both of which can cause injury.

In training the following tips will help:

- play with your dog before and after training.

- do not over train him. 5-10 minutes is enough, which can be gradually increased in the future to 20 minutes at a time.

- do not tease or laugh at your dog. Do not yell or hit him.

- use the same words each time you give a command, such as "Champ, sit".

- aim for gradual improvement over time. Your dog will often appear to take two steps forward and one step back. This is to be expected.

- don't lose your temper. Don't chase your dog, let him come to you.

- review the work already learned.

- reward with praise and pats, not tidbits except occasionally. Use a definite but happy tone of voice.

THE ABC'S OF OBEDIENCE

Obedience training is for control of your dog. I am reviewing the basic commands here for your information. You want automatic obedience,

SIT
To teach "sit", place your dog at your left side. Give the command "sit". Pull back on the collar and push down on the rump (not the spine) with your hand. When sitting say "good dog". Then walk forward and repeat the command.

HEEL
Heel means to stay on the left side of the trainer closely, even though the trainer is standing still. To teach "heel", hold the end of the leash in your right hand and hold left hand on leash close to the neck. Command to "heel" and start walking forward.

If dog pulls ahead or behind give a series of quick snaps to bring back to heel. A quick change of direction combined with a leash snap works well to get the dogs attention and bring him into line. Repeat command "heel" until he knows it means he must walk closely at your side. Praise him when he performs well.

HEEL OFF LEASH
When your dog has mastered "heel", try heeling off leash in an enclosed yard or area. To teach, command "heel" and start walking, stop and command "sit". If he runs away put him back on the leash and heel. Try again later.

COME
To teach the dog to come to you, take a long clothes line or cord and attach the end of it to the collar of the dog or puppy. Command "come". If he does not move pull him in steadily and make him sit in front of you. Then praise him as though he has done it himself. Try again.

When the dog comes on command, take the rope off. Try this in an enclosed area so he cannot run away.

Some dogs do not run away but keep a safe distance from the owner so they cannot be put back on leash, usually about 6-10 feet. You can get him to come running back to you by throwing something behind him when he is not looking. A rock or the leash itself will do the job.

DOWN
Start the dog from a "sit" command, then command "down" and shove down on the shoulders. Another method is to place the leash between the heel and sole of one of your shoes and pull up on the leash slowly, pulling the neck down. Repeat command "down". To assist, pull the front legs forward. Praise him.

SIT-STAY
"Stay" is most easily learned if combined with "sit". While sitting command "stay" while placing your left palm flat against his face. If he gets up force him

Walk around him. If he gets up say "no" and put him
back in the same spot.

Walk further away. If successful, walk out of sight.
If the dog gets up put back in the same spot and
repeat.

Finally, try the sit-stay when other dogs are present.

DOWN-STAY
Start with your dog in a down position. Command "stay"
while placing your left palm against his face flat.
If he gets up say "no" and return him to his position.

A chain training collar helps training since corrections can be made easily and effectively with the
leash. It is required for classes in obedience work.

If you train at home, vary the lessons and the conditions under which training is given. Take the
dog out to a field or park or beach for variety and
so that he will obey under all conditions and smells.

By training each dog individually, each is then ready
to then be an obedient member of a pack.

PACK TRAINING

All dogs in a group establish a social group and a
pecking order within the group. Whatever a strong or
dominant dog does in a group, the others will follow.
If one runs away the others probably will also. It
is important therefore that the dogs consider you
the alpha or leader of the pack so they will obey you.

To do this one key is to counteract dog dependence
in the pack by separating the dogs periodically,
taking them out separately, give them time alone with
you, and taking them into the house to socialize them.

When attempting to train several dogs together start with two animals, get their attention and repeat the command until they are familiar with it. such as "dogs come","dogs sit","dogs quiet", "down" or other commands. When two dogs work well together add a third and train together.

Tricks and group play in the yard are very important in getting the pack to relate to the owner and to perform on command. They can also be lots of fun for the pets.

Basic tricks are:

- "retrieving" a ball or article and returning it to the owner. Command "seek ball", "bring ball", and "drop it" or "out".

  With a pack it is fun to see who can find it first and bring it back.

- "jumping" over a stick or over a "hurdle" can be easily taught by walking the dog over the stick placed on the ground and then raising it slowly.

  Several dogs can also enjoy this jumping.

- "retrieving" can be combined with "jumping" by retrieving over a hurdle.

- dogs can be taught to run through barrels and hoops, playing catch can be done with several dogs at one time, and rolling over from a "down " position can be done, as well as running up and down a short flight of stairs.

With anything you attempt to do with your dogs, the same basic things apply...never do anything that has the potential to hurt your dogs, and make any corrections in the kindest way possible.

Remember, your dogs want your affection and love. They will eagerly try to do what will please you, the owner...especially if the result of doing otherwise is displeasing for them.

Never withdraw your love and praise from your dogs, never give up on their training, and be steady and consistent in your behavior with them for best results.

CONCLUSION

When you decide to bring a new dog or puppy into your home, you want to enjoy him and you want him to fit-in easily with the dog or dogs you already have.

To best attain this goal, you must understand dogs and why they behave the way they do. You must look at each dog as an individual, with breed characteristics and a personality of its own. Each of your dogs is an individual first and a member of a pack second. Some of those individual characteristics may need to be modified.

In addition, your multidog pack has group characteristics and social behaviors which also must be understood.

As a multidog owner and perhaps "back-yard breeder" you are their leader. You determine what happens to them in their environment on a daily basis.

As you strive to have "the best dogs you have ever had" remember that your dogs will develop a closeness and rapport with you if they have many daily personal contacts with you and others in the household.

In addition, you must devise a variable schedule to:
- attend to their basic physical needs for shelter, food, water, and health maintaince.

- exercise and play with them.

- socialize them through walks outside the yard and rides in the car to different places.

- supervise their changing lives and needs.

- monitor their well-being and provide protection when needed, as well as enough variety to alleviate daily boredom.

- provide the boundaries of their lives through training, leash training, and housebreaking.

- and, provide love and affection.

This books was written to provide tips for the multidog owner . By meeting the needs of the WHOLE dog, and seeking solutions to your day-to-day dog problems which are innovative but humane, you will certainly double your fun...and so will they.